DOOMED HISTORY

CRASHING IN FLAMES!

The *Hindenburg* Disaster, 1937

by Tim Cooke

BEARPORT
PUBLISHING

Minneapolis, Minnesota

Credits: Front Cover, ©Everett Historical/Shutterstock; 3, ©Rolf Mexiko/Public Domain; 4–5, ©U.S Navy/NARA; 5, ©Everett Historical/Shutterstock; 6, ©Everett Historical/ Shutterstock; 7t, ©Everett Collection/Shutterstock; 7b, ©Cunard White Star Line/Public Domain; 8, ©Imagentle/Shutterstock; 9, ©Everett Historical/Shutterstock; 10, ©Associated Press/Public Domain; 11, ©Lee Vasin/Shutterstock; 12, ©Christopher R. W. Nevinson/Public Domain; 13, ©Everett Collection/Shutterstock; 14, ©The Print Collector/ Alamy; 15t, ©Southern Methodist University, Central University Libraries, DeGoyler Library/Robert Yarnall Richie/Public Domain; 15b, ©National Air and Space Museum, Smithsonian; 16, ©Granger Historical Picture Archive/Alamy; 17, ©Everett Collection/ Shutterstock; 18, ©Everett Collection/Shutterstock; 19, ©Associated Press/Murray Becker/ Public Domain; 20, ©Pathe/William Deeke/Public Domain; 21, ©Everett Collection/ Shutterstock; 22, ©Everett Historical/Shutterstock; 23t, ©Everett Historical/Shutterstock; 23b, ©Paxswill/Public Domain; 24, ©Associated Press/Public Domain; 25, ©Everett Collection/Shutterstock; 26–27, ©Arquivo da FAB; O Cruzeiro, Rio de Janeiro/Jorge Kfuri/ Public Domain; 28, ©Bundesarchiv, B 145 Bild-P049500/CC-BY-SA 3.0/German Federal Archives; 29, ©Anton Volynets/Shutterstock.

Bearport Publishing Company Product Development Team
President: Jen Jenson; Director of Product Development: Spencer Brinker; Senior Editor: Allison Juda; Editor: Charly Haley; Associate Editor: Naomi Reich; Senior Designer: Colin O'Dea; Associate Designer: Elena Klinkner; Associate Designer: Kayla Eggert; Product Development Assistant: Anita Stasson

Brown Bear Books
Children's Publisher: Anne O'Daly; Design Manager: Keith Davis; Picture Manager: Sophie Mortimer

Library of Congress Cataloging-in-Publication Data is available at www.loc.gov or upon request from the publisher.

ISBN: 979-8-88509-395-8 (hardcover)
ISBN: 979-8-88509-517-4 (paperback)
ISBN: 979-8-88509-632-4 (ebook)

For more information, write to Bearport Publishing, 5357 Penn Avenue South, Minneapolis, MN 55419.

CONTENTS

A NEW WAY TO TRAVEL

On May 6, 1937, the future of aviation was changed forever. The world's largest airship had reached its destination in New Jersey. Just as the flight was ending, tragedy struck.

Just one year earlier, *Hindenburg* had made its first three-day **commercial** journey across the Atlantic Ocean. The airship flew from Germany to the United States, dazzling the world with its speed and style. It was hailed as the future of air transportation.

Hindenburg was more than 800 feet (240 m) long and cruised at about 80 miles per hour (130 kph).

The frames of airships like *Hindenburg* were largely made of light metals that were easier to lift off the ground.

Zeppelins

Hindenburg was the largest zeppelin, or **rigid** airship, ever built. It had a frame made from an aluminum **alloy**, which was then covered with a fabric balloon and filled with gas. Engines turned propellers to power the aircraft, and **rudders** allowed the huge craft to be steered.

Hindenburg

THE FIRST SIGNS OF TROUBLE

Hindenburg had made several successful flights between Germany and the United States. It had built up a reputation for speed and comfort, but there was danger below the balloon.

A journey on Hindenburg was intended to be a luxury experience. The passengers traveled comfortably in the aircraft's **hull**. They could spend their time in writing and reading rooms or taking in fresh air from seating areas with windows that opened up to the open sky all around. The airship even had walkways where the passengers could exercise.

The passengers also had their own cabins with twin bunks for sleeping.

Passengers had their meals served to them.

Life in the Sky

Passengers ate their meals in two dining rooms that served meals prepared by professional chefs. After dinner, many guests relaxed in a lounge—the only place on the aircraft where people were allowed to smoke. This room was sealed and **pressurized** to prevent any sparks from floating up to the balloon's fabric and setting it on fire.

ACROSS THE ATLANTIC

In the 1930s, flight was the fastest way to cross the Atlantic Ocean. The ocean liner *Queen Mary* could make the trip in five days. *Hindenburg's* record was just 43 hours. And, unlike on the *Queen Mary*, *Hindenburg's* passengers didn't get seasick!

A Safe and Cheap Gas

A fire on an airship would be a disaster. That's why the German designers of zeppelins originally filled them with helium—a gas that can lift ships but that does not burn. Germany originally bought the expensive gas from the United States.

Today, hot air balloons are controlled by burners that heat air within the balloons.

TWO GASES

Airships of the day were either filled with hydrogen or helium. Both gases are lighter than air. Hydrogen is cheaper and easier to get ahold of than helium. However, it is extremely **flammable**.

Switching to Hydrogen

In the mid-1930s, a politician named Adolf Hitler and his Nazi Party had seized control of Germany. Hitler threatened to start wars in Europe, so the United States stopped selling helium to Germany. America hoped to prevent the gas from being used for military purposes. The Germans decided to use hydrogen in their zeppelins instead. This included *Hindenburg*.

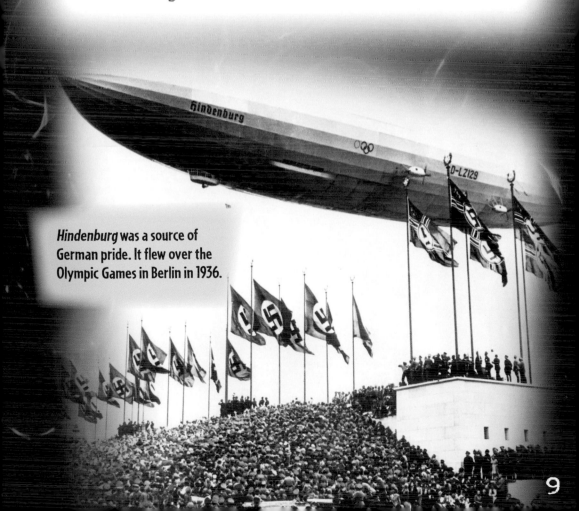

Hindenburg was a source of German pride. It flew over the Olympic Games in Berlin in 1936.

Stormy Weather

Hindenburg lifted off from Frankfurt, Germany, on the evening of May 3, 1937, carrying 36 passengers and 61 crew members. Its journey across the Atlantic Ocean was slowed by **headwinds**. The airship was hours behind schedule by the time it reached Boston, Massachusetts, just before noon on May 6. Then, thunderstorms meant Captain Max Pruss had to wait before flying over New York City. When the craft finally passed over, people rushed out of their homes and offices to catch a glimpse of the airship.

Traffic came to a standstill as people watched *Hindenburg* fly over Manhattan.

Thunderstorms made it too dangerous for *Hindenburg* to land as planned.

Flight over Manhattan

Weather, once again, delayed the journey as *Hindenburg* reached its final destination. The airship was due to land at Lakehurst, New Jersey, but continuing thunderstorms made it too dangerous. Instead, Pruss steered the zeppelin along New Jersey's beaches while he waited for the weather to clear. At 6:22 p.m., he was told the storms had passed and it was finally safe. The airship was now half a day late.

DISASTER STRIKES

Already behind schedule, Captain Pruss hoped to make up lost time with a quick landing before the planned return flight to Europe.

Usually, members of the public were allowed to look around a **moored** airship after its landing. But because of weather delays, there was no time to prolong the stop. The airship would have to be quickly landed, unloaded, and prepared for its return trip. Some passengers needed to get back for the **coronation** of Britian's King George VI.

RADIO TIMES

Price Twopence

King George VI was crowned in London, England, on May 12, 1937.

Hindenburg flies over the airfield at Lakehurst on an earlier flight.

The Final Approach

Captain Pruss started *Hindenburg's* final approach to the Lakehurst Naval Air Station in New Jersey at about 7:00 p.m. As the airship drew near the mooring mast, reporters and members of the public gathered to watch from below. The **ground crew** got ready to secure the airship once the onboard crew had lowered long ropes.

Tricky Landing

Pruss planned to make a landing **maneuver** called a flying moor. Crew aboard the airship would drop its ropes while they were still about 210 ft (65 m) up, and then workers on the ground would pull the craft down. *Hindenburg* had only landed this way a few times before, and this time it had trouble from the start. As Pruss approached the airfield, the ground crew was not ready to grab the mooring lines. So, the captain abandoned the landing.

Like other German vehicles of the time, *Hindenburg* had swastika flags, the symbols of the Nazi government.

Captain Pruss used equipment, including navigation devices, to pilot *Hindenburg*.

Another Try

A couple of minutes later, Pruss was ready to try again. He approached the mooring mast, but the airship was traveling too fast. Pruss put the rear engines in reverse to reduce the aircraft's speed, but something wasn't right. The huge balloon began to bob up and down.

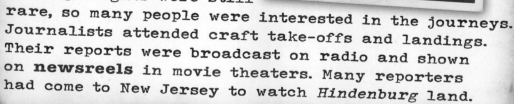

A MEDIA SHOW

Airship flights were still rare, so many people were interested in the journeys. Journalists attended craft take-offs and landings. Their reports were broadcast on radio and shown on **newsreels** in movie theaters. Many reporters had come to New Jersey to watch *Hindenburg* land.

Hindenburg flies over Lakehurst Naval Air Station as the captain prepares to land.

Countdown to Disaster

As the wind changed direction, Pruss turned left and right. The airship was swerving on its way toward the mooring mast. *Hindenburg* was wobbling with its nose sticking up. Pruss tried to steady *Hindenburg* by dumping hundreds of pounds of water from the ship, but the balloon remained unstable.

WATER BALLAST

Zeppelins carried large amounts of water. This **ballast** prevented the airship from floating up into the atmosphere.

Reaching for the Lines

Twenty-one minutes after *Hindenburg* started its final approach, the airship was about 300 ft (90 m) above the ground. The ship's crew dropped mooring lines from both sides of the airship. The ground crew caught hold of the lines from the **port** side and attached them to ropes on the ground. But they could not reach the **starboard** lines. As the airship moved in the wind, the port side lines stretched tighter and tighter.

Rain started to fall as the mooring lines were dropped, making the ground crew's job even more difficult.

Disaster!

While the crew struggled to moor the airship, people watching from nearby noticed that a part of Hindenburg's fabric covering was fluttering in the wind, as if it had been ripped. One onlooker said they saw a blue flame at the top rear of the zeppelin. No one knows for sure what happened, and none of the cameras recording the landing captured the exact moment disaster struck.

Hindenburg was close to the mooring mast when the rear of the airship burst into flames.

It took less than a minute before the entire ship was on fire.

Fireball

Suddenly, the airship was engulfed in flames. People on the ground watched in horror as the airship's 16 bags of hydrogen caught fire and exploded. The zeppelin plunged down, its tail hitting the ground first as flames roared out of its pointed front. *Hindenburg*'s fabric covering was soon covered in flames as its twisted metal frame hit the ground.

LIFE OR DEATH

As the fiery wreck plunged down, people on the ground closest to the ship ran for their lives.

The ground crew beneath the airship sprinted away as it fell. Those further away looked on in disbelief. The crowd included radio and newsreel reporters, as well as passengers who were waiting to fly back to Germany. Everything happened so quickly that no one could do anything to stop it.

As *Hindenburg* crashed, some people on board managed to escape from the cabin beneath the balloon.

Reporters at the airfield rushed to write their stories about the disaster.

Eyewitness

Herb Morrison was a radio announcer who was at Lakehurst to help record a newsreel showing *Hindenburg's* arrival. When the airship plunged to the ground in flames, Morrison's first thought was for the victims. The shock and sorrow in his report captured the horror of what was happening. For many who would watch the tragedy later, Morrison voiced what they were all thinking.

NEWSREELS

In the 1930s, televisions were still being developed. Most people got their news from newspapers, radios, or newsreels played at movie theaters. There were four newsreel teams at Lakehurst to film the landing, but none captured the moment the zepplin caught fire. They had all stopped filming after the ground crew caught the mooring ropes.

From Luxury Ride to Death

Hindenburg slammed to the ground in a huge ball of flames. The starboard side of the airship struck first, trapping passengers on that side under the crumbling wreckage that followed. Most of those who weren't trapped had been in the cabin beneath the balloon at the time of the disaster. They jumped from the fiery remains. In total, 13 passengers died.

The day after the disaster, the wreckage of the huge airship still smoldered.

Victims were flown back to Germany where officials of the Nazi Party honored their dead citizens.

Trapped Crew

In addition to the passengers that were killed, 22 crew members died in the crash. Most had been inside the airship's hull. They had no chance of escaping the intense heat of the flames speeding through the craft. One member of the ground crew also died when he couldn't get away from the crash in time.

A memorial marks the site where the airship crashed.

Young Survivors

The youngest crew member who made it through the disaster was 14-year-old cabin boy Werner Franz. The youngest passenger to survive, Werner Doehner, was returning home after a vacation with his family. He was only 8 at the time. Werner's father and sister were killed, but his mother and older brother survived.

THE LAST SURVIVOR

When Werner Doehner died in 2019, he was the last remaining survivor of the *Hindenburg* crash. For most of his life, he did not talk about the disaster. However, on the 80th anniversary, he explained how his mother saved him and his brother by throwing them out a window.

An Amazing Escape

Many of those who escaped the disaster were badly burned by the intense flames. Some had broken bones and other extreme injuries from the crash. The survivors were rushed to get the medical help they needed. Many spent months recovering in the hospital.

Injured but alive, shocked survivors of the disaster were led away to receive medical attention.

WHAT HAPPENED NEXT

Rigid airships had once been seen as the future of flight. But after the *Hindenburg* crash, many people were too scared to fly in them.

People immediately started to look for a cause of the disaster. Some experts believed a lightning bolt caused the fire. Others thought there must have been a gas leak or a rip in the airship's fabric. The most widely accepted theory was that **static electricity** had built up as the airship flew through thunderstorms that afternoon. The fabric of the airship acted as a **conductor** for this electricity. Then, a spark had **ignited** the hydrogen gas inside.

Sabotage?

Not everyone agreed with the static electricity theory. Pruss, who survived the crash, had been a pilot on zeppelins for nearly a decade. He had flown through many thunderstorms without any problems. Pruss believed *Hindenburg* was **sabotaged** in an attempt to embarrass the Nazi government in Germany.

WAS THERE A BOMB?

Captain Pruss accused passenger Joseph Spah of planting a bomb on *Hindenburg*. During the flight, Spah often visited the airship's freight room to feed his dog. Pruss claimed that during these visits Spah was actually building and hiding a bomb. There is no evidence to support this claim.

At the height of airships' popularity in the 1930s, different airships traveled all around the world.

People associated airships with Germany, which was becoming more warlike under Hitler and the Nazis.

The End of the Airship

The *Hindenburg* crash ended the brief era of passenger airships. Around the world, people were now terrified of flying on zeppelins. At the same time, tensions between Germany and the rest of the world were rising. People also stopped using the German zeppelins as a way of rejecting Hitler's Nazi government.

THE DEADLIEST DISASTER

The *Hindenburg* crash was not the deadliest airship disaster. On April 4, 1933, the USS *Akron*, a helium-filled U.S. Navy airship, went down during bad weather. The crash killed 76 crew members, leaving only 3 survivors.

A New Dawn

Before the disaster, there had been a growing interest among the public for air travel. Flying was much faster and more comfortable than sea travel for long trips. The crash of *Hindenburg* changed the face of aviation, as engineers abandoned airships in order to focus instead on building large airplanes to carry passengers. The disaster ultimately paved the way for safer forms of transportation—modern airplanes.

The first jet airliners came into service in the early 1950s.

KEY DATES

1936

March *Hindenburg* makes its first commercial flight.

1937

May 3 *Hindenburg* leaves Frankfurt, Germany, heading for the United States on what will be its final trip.

May 6

shortly before noon *Hindenburg* flies over Boston.

afternoon Bad weather delays the flight. It eventually makes its way through New York and up the New Jersey shoreline.

6:22 p.m. *Hindenburg* is given the all-clear to land.

7:00 p.m. *Hindenburg* begins its final approach to Lakehurst Naval Air Station.

7:09 p.m. Captain Pruss begins to maneuver *Hindenburg* for landing.

7:14 p.m. Pruss puts the engines in reverse to slow the airship.

7:18 p.m. Pruss drops water ballast to steady *Hindenburg*.

7:21 p.m. *Hindenburg* drops its mooring lines.

7:25 p.m. Witnesses see a flutter in the fabric of the airship, followed by a fireball as the balloon catches fire. *Hindenburg* crashes to the ground less than a minute later.

QUIZ How much have you learned about the *Hindenburg* disaster? It's time to test your knowledge! Then, check your answers on page 32.

1. **What gas was used for *Hindenburg's* final flight?**
   a) helium
   b) hydrogen
   c) oxygen

2. **Where did *Hindenburg* take off from on May 3, 1938?**
   a) Berlin
   b) Munich
   c) Frankfurt

3. **What was *Hindenburg's* record for crossing the Atlantic?**
   a) 43 hours
   b) 24 hours
   c) 96 hours

4. **Why did *Hindenburg* reach its destination late?**
   a) bad weather
   b) an emergency landing for a sick passenger
   c) the captain got lost

5. **How many people on the ground died in the disaster?**
   a) 0
   b) 1
   c) 15

GLOSSARY

alloy a mixture of metals

ballast heavy material carried in a ship or airship to make it more stable

commercial a product or service for the public sold in order to make money

conductor something that can transmit or carry electricity

coronation a ceremony to crown a new king or queen

flammable able to easily catch fire

ground crew people who assist aircraft from the ground

headwinds winds blowing against the direction in which a ship is traveling

hull the frame or body of a boat or airship

ignited started burning

maneuver a difficult movement that requires planning and skill

moored tied up to a fixed point, such as an anchor or a post

newsreels short movies that report news and current events

port the left-hand side of a ship or aircraft

pressurized sealed to keep the air pressure inside a space the same as the pressure at Earth's surface

rigid stiff and difficult to bend

rudders blades used to steer a boat or aircraft

sabotaged deliberately damaged or destroyed as a form of attack or to create panic and confusion

starboard the right-hand side of a ship or aircraft

static electricity electricity that builds up in an object as a result of friction and that is eventually released as a series of sparks

INDEX

READ MORE

Kortemeier, Todd. *Air France Flight 447* (Engineering Disasters). Minneapolis: Abdo Publishing, 2020.

McCollum, Sean. *Fighting to Survive Airplane Crashes: Terrifying True Stories* (*Fighting to Survive*). North Mankato, MN: Compass Point Books, 2020.

O'Daly, Anne. *Sunken Ship of Dreams! The Titanic, 1912* (Doomed History). Minneapolis: Bearport Publishing, 2022.

LEARN MORE ONLINE

1. Go to **www.factsurfer.com** or scan the QR code below.

2. Enter **"Crashing in Flames"** into the search box.

3. Click on the cover of this book to see a list of websites.

Answers to the quiz on page 30

1) B; 2) C; 3) A; 4) A; 5) B